OWN YOUR
STORY

MAKE
TODAY
AMAZING

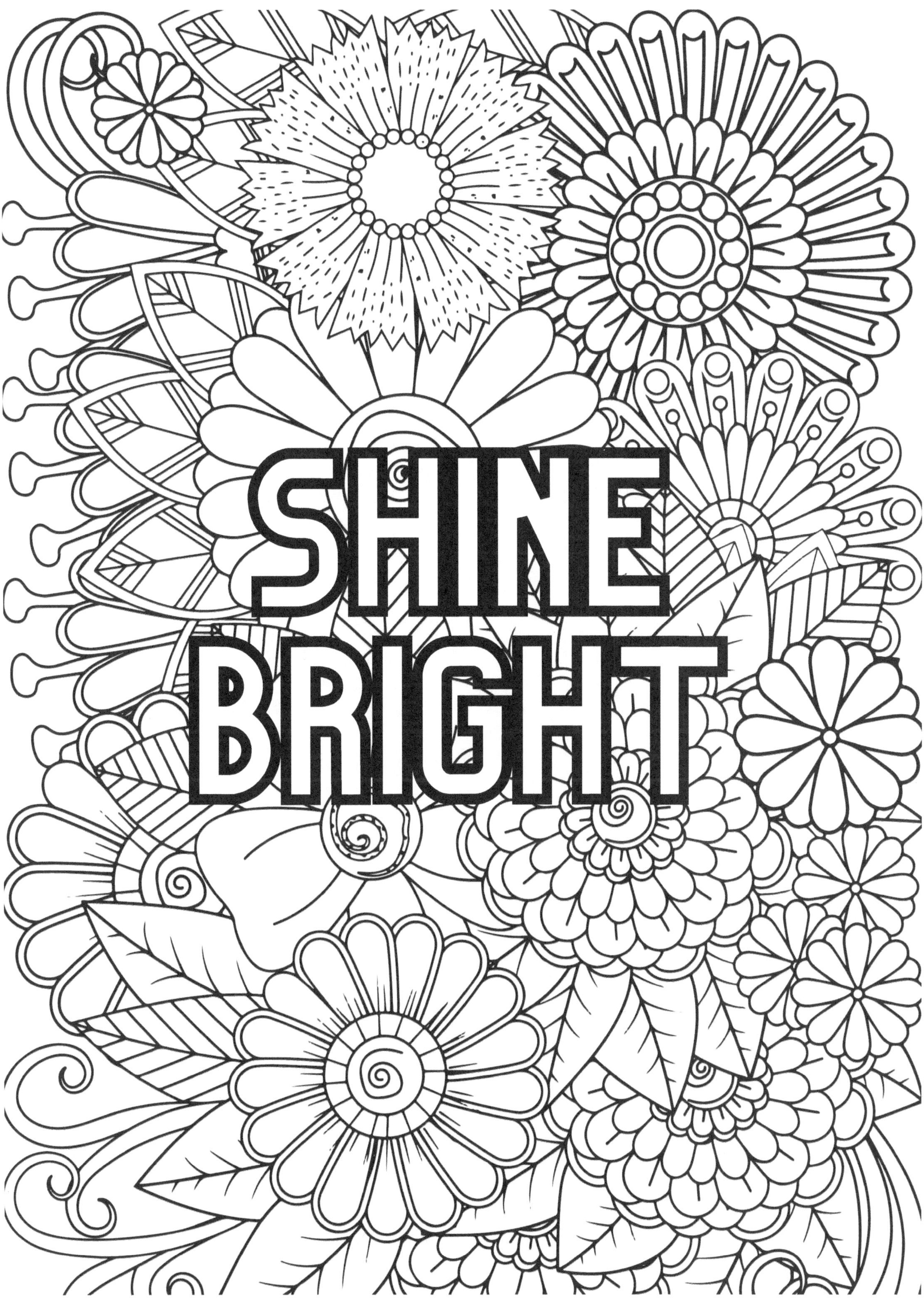
SHINE
BRIGHT

BELIEVE,
ACHIEVE

DO EPIC
THINGS

KEEP IT
REAL

STAY
TRUE, BE
YOU

RISE AND
SHINE

LIVE WITH
PASSION

KEEP
MOVING
FORWARD

BE
BRAVE

YOU
MATTER

STAY
UNSTOPPABLE

DARE TO
DREAM

SEIZE THE
DAY

YOU'VE
GOT THIS

DREAM BIG,
WORK
HARD

LIVE
BOLDLY

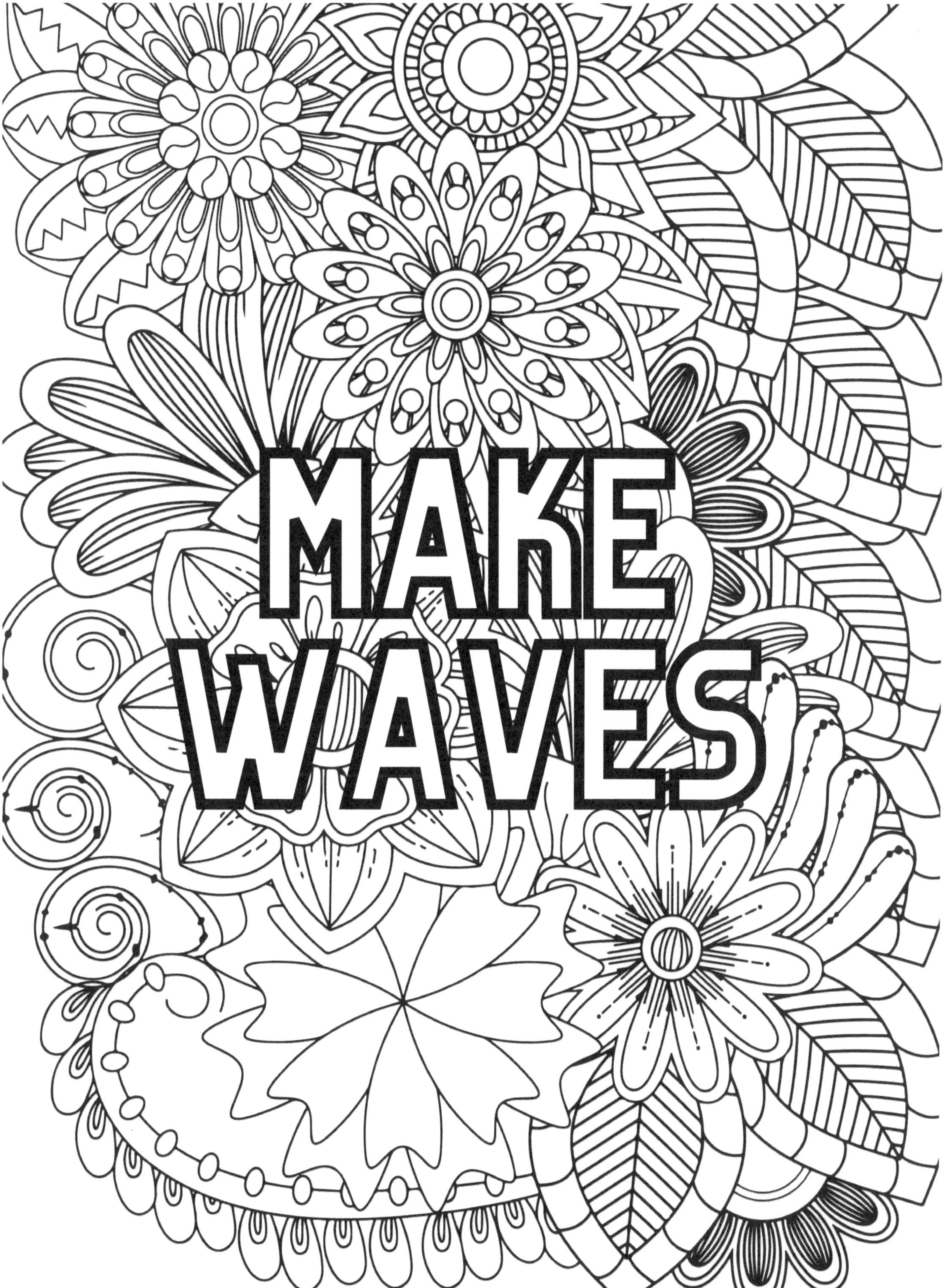
MAKE
WAVES

SEEK
ADVENTURE

YOU CAN

THINK BIG

STAY
FOCUSED

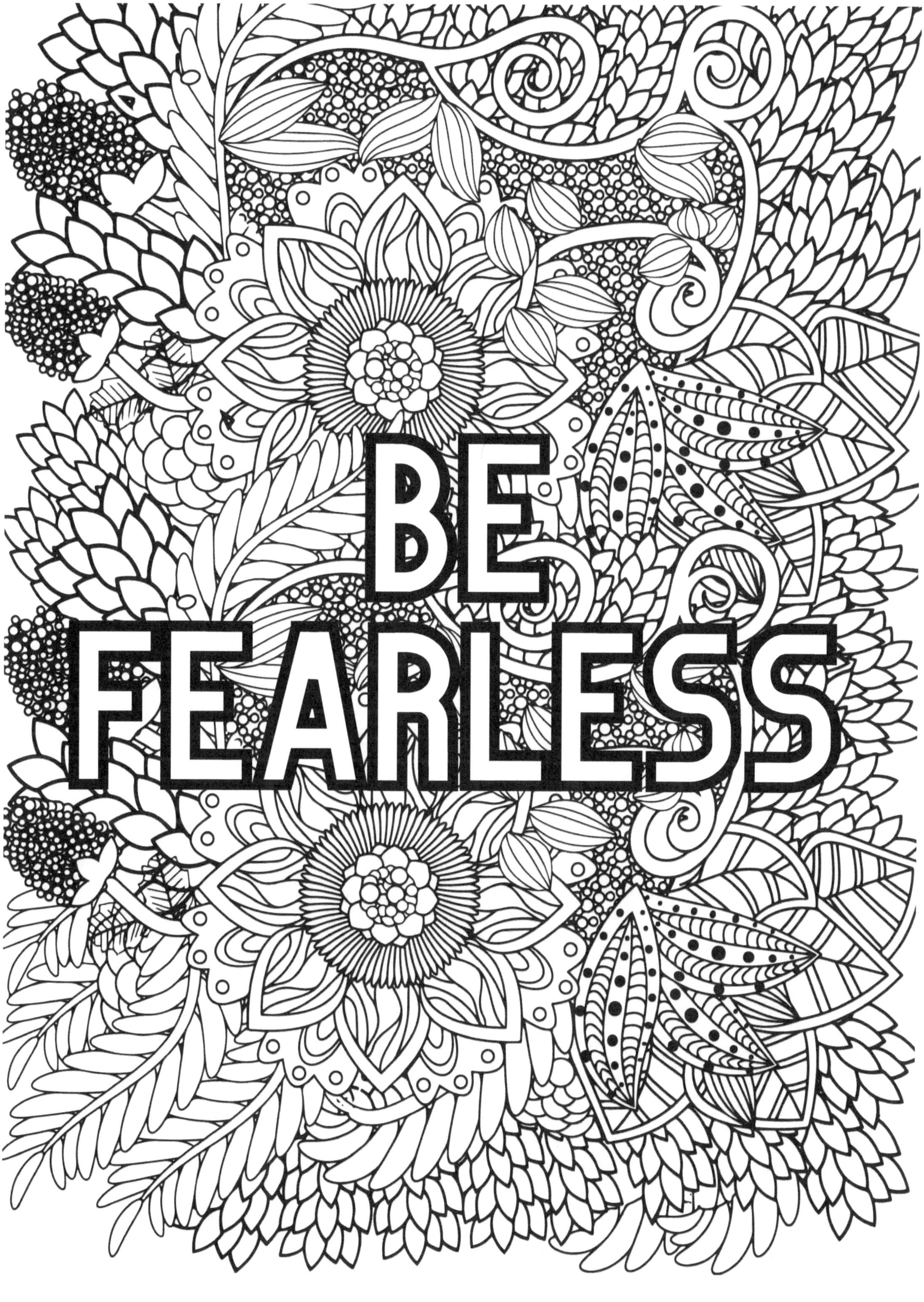
BE
FEARLESS

STAND
OUT

SHINE
BRIGHT

EXPLORE,
DISCOVER

LEARN,
GROW

INSPIRE
OTHERS

SPARK
PASSION

Made in United States
Troutdale, OR
07/18/2024

21355650R00038